How to Improve Lead Generation

Practical Guide

A. Luvaren

Practical Guide

1.Introduction

Market and lead generation represent a crucial element for the success of modern businesses. In an increasingly competitive and digitalized commercial landscape, the ability to attract, engage, and convert potential customers is essential for ensuring sustainable growth. Lead generation, in particular, is the process of identifying and capturing potential customers (leads) interested in the products or services offered by the company. Market generation, on the other hand, involves expanding the company's presence in new market segments or increasing its share in existing ones.

Importance of Market Generation

Expansion of Customer Base: Market generation is essential for expanding the customer base. Penetrating new market segments means reaching customers who may not be aware of the company's products or services. This process helps diversify risks and stabilize revenues, reducing dependence on a single market.

Competitive Advantage: An effective market generation strategy can provide a significant competitive advantage. Companies that can identify and penetrate new markets before their competitors can establish a dominant presence and build customer loyalty before other companies can enter the same market.

Revenue Growth: Market generation can lead to increased sales and revenue. Penetrating new markets or expanding presence in existing ones allows reaching new consumer groups, thus increasing the company's earning potential.

Innovation and Adaptability: The need to enter new markets drives companies to innovate and adapt. This push for creativity can lead to the development of new products or services and the adoption of new technologies or business practices that can improve overall efficiency and effectiveness.

Importance of Lead Generation

Identification of Potential Customers: Lead generation allows companies to identify and nurture potential customers interested in their products or services. This process helps focus sales and marketing efforts on individuals or businesses that have already shown interest, increasing the chances of conversion.

Optimization of Sales and Marketing Resources: With an effective lead generation system, sales and marketing resources can be used more efficiently. Instead of trying to sell to a generic audience, the company can focus on qualified leads, optimizing time and resources and improving return on investment.

Sustainable Growth: Lead generation is a key component for sustainable growth. A constant flow of new leads allows the company to maintain a full sales pipeline, ensuring that there are always new customers ready to be converted, regardless of seasonal or economic fluctuations.

Customer Retention and Upselling: Lead generation doesn't stop with acquiring new customers; it is also crucial for retention and upselling. Identifying leads among existing customers allows promoting new products or services, increasing the customer's lifetime value and overall satisfaction.

Fundamentals of Market Generation

Market Analysis

Market Research: Market research is the first step in market generation. This process involves collecting and analyzing data related to potential customers, industry trends, competitors, and economic conditions. Tools like surveys, focus groups, secondary data analysis, and market analysis software are used to gain a deep understanding of the market.

Market Segmentation: Once market

information is collected, it's important to segment the market based on various criteria such as demographics, buying behavior, needs, and preferences. Market segmentation helps identify the most promising segments and develop targeted marketing strategies for each segment.

SWOT Analysis: SWOT (Strengths, Weaknesses, Opportunities, Threats) analysis is a crucial tool for evaluating the company's position in the market. Identifying internal strengths and weaknesses, as well as external opportunities and threats, allows developing effective strategies for market generation.

Development of Market Strategy

Positioning: Clearly defining the company's positioning in the market is essential. Positioning relates to the perception that consumers have of the company and its products or services compared to the competition. A distinctive positioning can attract the right customers and differentiate the company in the market.

Value Proposition: The value proposition is a clear statement explaining why customers should choose the company's products or services. This proposition must address the needs and desires of the target customers, offering solutions that competitors cannot provide.

Marketing Mix: Developing an effective marketing mix, also known as the 4 Ps (Product, Price, Place, Promotion), is essential for market generation. Each element of the mix must be carefully planned and coordinated to maximize market impact.

Execution of Market Strategy

Marketing Campaigns: Creating and executing targeted marketing campaigns is a key component of market generation. These campaigns can include advertising, promotions, events, digital marketing, and more. The goal is to reach target market segments and effectively communicate the company's value proposition.

Strategic Partnerships: Collaborating with other companies or organizations can expand market reach and offer new growth opportunities. Strategic partnerships can include joint ventures, distribution agreements, marketing collaborations, and more.

Measurement and Optimization: Measuring the results of marketing campaigns is essential to evaluate the effectiveness of the market generation strategy. Using analytics tools to monitor performance and continuously improve based on collected data.

Fundamentals of Lead Generation

Identification of Leads

Target Definition: Clearly defining who the ideal leads are is the first step in lead generation. This involves creating detailed buyer personas that represent the target customer segments. These profiles include demographic data, behaviors, needs, goals, and challenges.

Lead Magnet: A lead magnet is a value offer that attracts potential customers and encourages them to provide their contact information. Examples of lead magnets include ebooks, webinars, free trials, whitepapers, exclusive discounts, and more. The goal is to offer something useful and relevant that prompts potential customers to engage with the company.

Lead Capture

Contact Forms and Landing Pages: Contact forms and landing pages are crucial tools for capturing leads. Landing pages should be optimized for conversion, with an attractive design, persuasive content, and a clear call to action. Contact forms should request only essential information to minimize abandonment.

SEO and Content Marketing: Search engine optimization (SEO) and content marketing are effective strategies to attract organic traffic and capture leads. Creating high-quality, keyword-optimized content can increase the company's visibility in search results and attract interested potential customers.

Paid Advertising: Paid advertising campaigns, such as Google Ads and social media ads, can generate a steady flow of qualified leads. These campaigns need to be well-planned and targeted to maximize return on investment.

Lead Nurturing

Email Marketing: Email marketing is one of the most effective tools for lead nurturing. Creating segmented and personalized email marketing campaigns can keep leads engaged and push them towards conversion. Automated email sequences can help nurture leads over time, providing valuable content and relevant offers.

CRM and Marketing Automation: Using a customer relationship management (CRM) system and marketing automation tools can improve the efficiency of lead generation and nurturing. These tools allow tracking interactions with leads, segmenting them, and automating communications based on their behavior and preferences.

Lead Scoring: Lead scoring is a technique that assigns a score to leads based on their likelihood of conversion. This process helps identify the most promising leads and focus sales efforts on them. Lead scoring is based on criteria such as browsing behavior, email interactions, demographics, and more.

Lead Conversion

Sales Funnel: A well-defined sales funnel is essential to guide leads through the purchase process. This funnel should be designed to meet the needs of leads at each stage of their journey, providing the information and resources needed to make an informed purchase decision.

Closing Sales: Sales closing techniques are fundamental to converting leads into customers. These techniques include handling objections, building trust and credibility, creating a sense of urgency, and offering purchase incentives. A well-trained and motivated sales team is essential for success in this phase.

Post-Sale Follow-Up: Post-sale follow-up is crucial to ensure customer satisfaction and encourage positive word-of-mouth. This phase includes customer support, technical support, satisfaction surveys, and upselling and cross-selling strategies.

Market and lead generation is a complex and multifaceted process that requires strategic planning, the use of advanced technologies, and continuous adaptation to changing market dynamics. The importance of these processes cannot be underestimated, as they are essential for acquiring new customers, expanding market presence, and ensuring sustainable company growth. By implementing effective market and lead generation strategies, companies can achieve their business goals and build lasting customer relationships, ensuring long-term success.

2.Difference between Market Generation and Lead Generation

Market Generation

Market generation refers to the process of expanding a company's presence within new markets or existing market segments. This strategy involves activities such as market research and analysis, identifying new opportunities, developing products and services suitable for new segments, and implementing targeted marketing strategies.

Lead Generation

Lead generation is the process of attracting and converting individuals or organizations interested in the company's products or services into potential customers (leads). This process includes identifying the target audience, using marketing techniques to capture their attention, and collecting contact information to nurture and eventually convert them into customers.

Main Models of Market Generation

1. **Geographic Expansion**: This model involves entering new geographic markets, both nationally and internationally. The company analyzes market opportunities, trends, and local regulations to adapt its products and marketing strategies.

2. **Product Diversification**: The company develops new products or services to attract new market segments. This can include innovating existing products or creating entirely new product lines to meet unmet needs.

3. **Market Segmentation**: This model focuses on identifying and targeting specific market segments that have not been previously exploited. The company analyzes

the demographic, psychographic, and behavioral characteristics of consumers to develop targeted strategies.

4. **Partnerships and Collaborations**: Companies can enter new markets through strategic partnerships, joint ventures, or collaborations with other companies already present in the target market. This approach allows sharing resources and expertise to penetrate new markets more effectively.

5. **Acquisitions and Mergers**: Acquiring or merging with other companies can be a quick way to enter new markets. This approach allows the acquisition of market share, expertise, and existing resources.

Lead Generation Strategy

What is a Lead?

A lead is an individual or organization that has shown interest in a company's products or services through a specific interaction or behavior. Leads are potential customers who can be converted into actual customers through the sales process.

Types of Leads

1. **Cold Leads**: These are individuals who have not yet shown active interest in the company or its products. These leads might have been obtained through outbound marketing activities such as cold calls or untargeted advertisements.

2. **Warm Leads**: These leads have shown some level of interest, such as visiting the company's website, downloading an ebook, or subscribing to a newsletter. They are more likely to convert compared to cold leads.

3. **Hot Leads**: These are individuals who have shown significant and immediate interest in the company and its products. They may have requested a product demo, participated in a webinar, or contacted the company directly for more information.

4. **Marketing Qualified Leads (MQL)**: These leads have interacted with the company's marketing and have been identified as potentially interested. They are ready to be passed to the sales team for further nurturing and conversion.

5. **Sales Qualified Leads (SQL)**: These leads have been assessed and deemed ready for direct interaction with the sales team. They have a high potential for conversion into paying customers.

Setting Lead Generation Goals

1. **Increase Lead Volume**: One of the

primary goals is to generate a larger volume of leads. This can be measured through metrics such as the number of new contacts acquired over a specific period.

2. **Improve Lead Quality**: Not all leads are created equal. Improving lead quality means attracting potential customers who are more likely to convert and who are better suited to the company's products or services.

3. **Optimize Conversion Rate**: Improving the conversion rate of leads into customers is a crucial goal. This can be achieved through lead nurturing strategies, personalized marketing, and sales funnel optimization.

4. **Reduce Cost per Lead**: An important financial goal is to reduce the cost associated with generating each lead. This can be achieved through optimizing marketing campaigns and using more effective channels.

5. **Increase ROI on Lead Generation Campaigns**: The ultimate goal is to maximize the return on investment of lead generation activities. This involves effectively managing marketing and sales resources to derive the most value from generated leads.

Lead Generation Techniques

1. **Content Marketing**: Creating and distributing valuable content, such as blogs, ebooks, whitepapers, videos, and infographics, to attract and engage potential customers. Content marketing helps educate the target audience and build trust with leads.

2. **SEO (Search Engine Optimization)**: Optimizing the website and content for search engines to improve organic visibility and attract qualified traffic. Using relevant keywords, creating quality content, and technical site optimization are fundamental.

3. **Email Marketing**: Using email marketing campaigns to nurture and engage leads. Emails can be personalized and segmented to provide relevant content and offers to leads at different stages of the sales funnel.

4. **Social Media Marketing**: Leveraging social media platforms to reach and engage potential customers. Social media campaigns can include organic posts, paid advertisements, and interactions with the audience to build relationships and attract leads.

5. **Webinars and Online Events**: Organizing webinars and online events to educate and engage the target audience. These events offer the opportunity to interact directly with leads and demonstrate the company's expertise.

6. **Pay-Per-Click Advertising (PPC)**: Using paid advertising campaigns on search

engines and social platforms to quickly reach a broad and qualified audience. PPC campaigns need to be well-targeted and optimized to maximize ROI.

7. **Referral Marketing**: Encouraging existing customers to refer new leads to the company. Referral marketing leverages existing trust and relationships to generate qualified leads.

8. **Influencer Marketing**: Collaborating with industry influencers to promote the company's products or services. Influencers can help reach new market segments and build credibility.

The difference between market generation and lead generation lies in the focus and strategies used. Market generation focuses on expanding the company into new market segments, while lead generation focuses on attracting and converting potential customers. Both strategies are crucial for the long-term success of the company and must be implemented with strategic planning and effective use of available resources."

3.Lead Generation

Lead generation is a fundamental process for any marketing strategy. It involves attracting and converting individuals interested in the products or services offered by a company into potential customers (leads). This process encompasses various techniques and channels, each playing a significant role in attracting and nurturing these contacts until their conversion into actual customers.

Content Marketing

Definition and Importance

Content marketing is a strategy based on creating and distributing valuable, relevant, and consistent content to attract and engage a well-defined target audience. The goal is to guide potential customers through the sales funnel by providing useful and relevant information that addresses their needs and questions.

Types of Content

1. **Blog Posts**: Informative articles that cover topics of interest to the target audience. Blogs are effective for improving organic visibility through search engine optimization (SEO).

2. **Ebooks and Whitepapers**: In-depth resources that provide detailed information on specific topics. These materials are often used as lead magnets in exchange for the readers' contact information.

3. **Infographics**: Visual representations of complex data and information. Infographics are easy to share and can increase engagement on social media.

4. **Videos**: Video content can range from

tutorials and product demonstrations to interviews and customer testimonials. Videos are particularly effective for capturing attention and conveying information in an engaging way.

5. **Case Studies**: Detailed stories of how a product or service has helped a customer solve a specific problem. Case studies are useful for demonstrating the effectiveness and value of the solutions offered.

Content Distribution

1. **Website and Blog**: Publishing content on your own website and blog is fundamental for attracting organic traffic and establishing the company as an authority in the industry.

2. **Social Media**: Sharing content on social media helps reach a wider audience and promotes interaction with potential customers.

3. **Email Marketing**: Sending personalized content through email marketing campaigns can keep the audience engaged and promote further interactions.

4. **Guest Posting**: Publishing content on third-party blogs and websites to reach new audience segments and increase the authority of your brand.

SEO and SEM

SEO (Search Engine Optimization)

Search engine optimization (SEO) is a strategy aimed at improving the organic visibility of a website in search engine results. A good SEO strategy involves various techniques and best practices that help search engines better understand the site's content and position it more favorably.

1. **Keyword Research**: Identifying relevant keywords that the target audience uses to search for information related to the products or services offered. Tools like Google Keyword Planner, Ahrefs, and SEMrush are useful for this activity.

2. **On-Page Optimization**: Including the identified keywords in page titles, meta descriptions, URLs, and content. Also optimizing the technical elements of the site, such as loading speed and internal link structure.

3. **Creating Quality Content**: Producing informative and valuable content that answers the questions and needs of the target audience. Quality content tends to be shared and obtain backlinks, further improving organic visibility.

4. **Backlinking**: Obtaining links from authoritative and relevant sites that point to your site. Backlinks are an important factor

for search engine ranking.

5. **Technical SEO**: Optimizing the technical aspects of the site, such as site structure, mobile usability, structured data, and robots.txt files. A technically optimized site is easier for search engines to index and navigate.

SEM (Search Engine Marketing)

Search engine marketing (SEM) includes both SEO and paid advertising (PPC) campaigns. The goal of SEM is to improve visibility in search engines through both organic and paid results.

1. **Google Ads**: Creating paid ad campaigns on Google Ads to appear in sponsored search results. Google Ads offers various ad formats, such as text ads, display ads, and shopping ads.

2. **Bing Ads**: Although less popular than Google, Bing Ads is an effective advertising platform that can reach a different and less competitive audience.

3. **Remarketing**: Using remarketing to show ads to visitors who have already interacted with the website. This helps keep the brand in the minds of potential customers and encourages them to complete a purchase.

4. **Performance Analysis**: Monitoring and analyzing the performance of SEM campaigns to continuously optimize ads, keywords, and budget. Tools like Google Analytics and Google Ads dashboards provide useful data for these analyses.

Social Media Marketing

Definition and Importance

Social media marketing is the use of social media platforms to promote a product, service, or brand. This strategy is essential for building brand awareness, engaging with the target audience, and generating leads.

Major Platforms

1. **Facebook**: One of the largest and most diverse platforms, ideal for targeting a broad audience through organic content and paid advertising.

2. **Instagram**: Great for visual content like photos and videos. Particularly effective for brands in the fashion, lifestyle, and food industries.

3. **LinkedIn**: A professional platform perfect for B2B marketing. Ideal for sharing professional content, thought leadership articles, and networking.

4. **Twitter**: Excellent for quick updates, news, and real-time interactions with the audience. Also used for customer service and engagement with followers.

5. **YouTube**: The primary platform for video content. Useful for tutorials, product reviews, webinars, and other forms of engaging video content.

Social Media Marketing Strategies

1. **Content Creation**: Develop an editorial plan that includes various types of content (texts, images, videos, stories) and that responds to the interests of the target audience.

2. **Paid Advertising**: Use the paid advertising tools of social media platforms to reach a specific audience through targeted ads. Targeting options include demographics, interests, behaviors, and connections.

3. **Engagement and Interaction**: Respond to comments, questions, and messages from the audience. Active interaction helps build a loyal community and improve brand perception.

4. **Performance Monitoring**: Use analytics tools to monitor performance metrics such as engagement, reach, clicks, and conversions. These data help optimize social media marketing strategies.

5. **Influencer Collaborations**: Partner with industry influencers to promote products or services. Influencers can increase brand visibility and generate qualified leads.

Email Marketing

Definition and Importance

Email marketing is a direct communication

strategy that uses email to send promotional and informational messages to a target audience. It is one of the most effective tools for lead generation, lead nurturing, and customer retention.

Types of Emails

1. **Newsletters**: Regular emails that provide updates, news, and valuable content to subscribers. Newsletters help keep the audience engaged and informed.

2. **Promotional Emails**: Messages that promote special offers, discounts, product launches, and other incentives to encourage purchases.

3. **Welcome Emails**: Messages sent to new subscribers to welcome them and introduce them to the brand. These emails set a positive tone and provide useful information about the next steps.

4. **Follow-up Emails**: Messages sent after a specific interaction, such as attending a webinar or downloading an ebook. These emails help maintain contact and push leads towards conversion.

5. **Cart Abandonment Emails**: Messages sent to customers who have abandoned their cart without completing the purchase. These emails often offer incentives to complete the purchase.

Best Practices for Email Marketing

1. **Personalization**: Use the recipient's name and personalize the email content based on their preferences and behaviors. Personalization increases engagement and the likelihood of conversion.

2. **Segmentation**: Divide the email list into segments based on demographics,

behaviors, and interests. Segmentation allows you to send more relevant and targeted messages.

3. **Valuable Content**: Provide useful and relevant content that addresses the needs of the audience. Avoid sending purely promotional emails.

4. **Clear Call to Action (CTA)**: Include clear and visible CTAs that guide recipients towards the desired action, such as visiting the website, downloading an ebook, or making a purchase.

5. **A/B Testing**: Experiment with different versions of emails to understand which elements (subject, CTA, images, etc.) work best. Use test results to optimize future campaigns.

Events and Trade Shows

Importance of Events and Trade Shows

Events and trade shows represent a unique opportunity to meet potential customers, partners, and other industry stakeholders face-to-face. Participating in these events increases brand visibility, generates qualified leads, and builds lasting relationships.

Types of Events

1. **Industry Trade Shows**: Events specific to the industry where companies showcase their products and services. Trade shows offer the opportunity to demonstrate solutions to a targeted audience and establish direct contacts with potential customers.

2. **Conferences and Summits**: Events that bring together industry experts to discuss the latest trends and innovations. Participating as a sponsor or speaker can increase the brand's authority and credibility.

3. **Workshops and Seminars**: Educational events where participants can learn new skills and knowledge. Organizing workshops can help demonstrate the company's expertise and generate qualified leads.

4. **Networking Events**: Events dedicated to networking and relationship building. These events are ideal for meeting new contacts and establishing strategic partnerships.

Strategies for Generating Leads at Events

1. **Attractive Booths**: Create a visually appealing booth that attracts visitors. Use banners, interactive displays, and product demonstrations to engage participants.

2. **Special Offers and Giveaways**: Offer special discounts, free samples, or gadgets in exchange for participants' contact information. Giveaways encourage visitors to leave their

details.

3. **Personal Interactions**: Interact directly with participants, answer their questions, and provide detailed information about products or services. Personal interactions help build trust relationships.

4. **Contact Collection**: Use tools like badge scanners or registration forms to collect participants' contact information. Ensure compliance with all privacy and GDPR regulations.

5. **Post-Event Follow-up**: Send follow-up emails to contacts collected during the event to maintain the relationship and push them towards further interactions and conversions.

Webinars and Live

Demos

Definition and Importance

Webinars and live demos are online events that provide an interactive platform to present products, services, and educational content to a targeted audience. These events are highly effective for generating qualified leads and demonstrating expertise in the field.

Types of Webinars and Live Demos

1. **Product Demonstrations**: Detailed presentations of how a product or service works. These webinars help potential customers understand the benefits and functionalities of the solution offered.

2. **Educational Webinars**: Informative sessions that provide valuable knowledge on specific topics. These webinars position the company as an industry authority and attract leads interested in learning more.

3. **Q&A Sessions**: Interactive sessions where participants can ask questions and receive real-time answers. These webinars engage the audience and address their specific concerns.

4. **Panel Discussions**: Webinars that bring together multiple experts to discuss a particular topic. Panel discussions offer varied perspectives and attract a broader audience.

Strategies for Generating Leads Through Webinars and Live Demos

1. **Promotion and Registration**: Promote the event through various channels, such as email marketing, social media, and the company website. Use a registration form to collect participants' contact information.

2. **Engaging Content**: Create compelling and valuable content that addresses the

interests and needs of the target audience. Use slides, videos, and interactive elements to keep participants engaged.

3. **Live Interaction**: Encourage interaction during the webinar through polls, Q&A sessions, and chat features. Interactive elements increase participant engagement and provide valuable feedback.

4. **Follow-up Emails**: Send follow-up emails to participants after the event to thank them for their attendance and provide additional resources. Follow-up emails help maintain the relationship and move leads further down the sales funnel.

5. **Recorded Content**: Record the webinar and make it available on-demand for those who could not attend live. On-demand content continues to generate leads over time.

Paid Advertising

Definition and Importance

Paid advertising involves the use of paid media channels to promote products, services, or content to a specific audience. This strategy allows for targeted reach and quick visibility, making it an essential component of lead generation.

Types of Paid Advertising

1. **Pay-Per-Click (PPC) Ads**: Ads that appear in search engine results or on partner websites. Advertisers pay a fee each time someone clicks on their ad. Google Ads and Bing Ads are popular PPC platforms.

2. **Social Media Ads**: Paid ads on social media platforms like Facebook, Instagram, LinkedIn, and Twitter. These ads can be targeted based on demographics, interests, behaviors, and connections.

3. **Display Ads**: Visual ads that appear on websites, apps, and social media. Display ads are effective for increasing brand awareness and retargeting previous visitors.

4. **Native Ads**: Ads that blend in with the content of the website or platform they appear on. Native ads are less intrusive and can provide a better user experience.

5. **Video Ads**: Ads that appear before, during, or after video content on platforms like YouTube and social media. Video ads are highly engaging and can convey complex messages effectively.

Strategies for Effective Paid Advertising

1. **Targeting and Segmentation**: Use precise targeting options to reach the right audience. Segmenting the audience allows for more relevant and personalized ad campaigns.

2. **Compelling Ad Copy and Creatives**: Create engaging ad copy and visuals that capture the audience's attention. Highlight the unique selling points and benefits of the product or service.

3. **Landing Pages**: Direct traffic from ads to dedicated landing pages optimized for conversions. Ensure that landing pages are relevant to the ad content and include a clear CTA.

4. **A/B Testing**: Test different versions of ads, targeting options, and landing pages to identify what works best. Use the insights gained to optimize future campaigns.

5. **Performance Monitoring and Optimization**: Continuously monitor the performance of paid advertising campaigns. Use analytics tools to track key metrics and make data-driven adjustments to improve results.

Lead generation is a multifaceted process that requires a strategic and integrated approach. By leveraging various techniques and channels such as content marketing, SEO, social media marketing, email marketing, events, webinars, and paid advertising, businesses can effectively attract and convert potential customers. Each strategy has its own strengths and should be tailored to the specific goals and target audience of the company. The key to successful lead generation is consistent effort, optimization, and a deep understanding of the audience's needs and behaviors.

4.Tools for Lead Generation

Lead generation is a complex process that requires the use of various tools to attract, manage, and convert potential customers. The tools available today are sophisticated and offer a wide range of features that simplify marketers' work, improving the efficiency and effectiveness of their campaigns.

In this section, we will explore in detail the main tools for lead generation, divided into four categories: CRM and lead management, marketing automation platforms, analytics and reporting tools, and social media management.

CRM and Lead Management

Definition and Importance

Customer Relationship Management (CRM) is a system that allows companies to manage

49

interactions with current and potential customers. CRMs are essential for lead generation because they help organize, automate, and synchronize sales, marketing, customer service, and technical support.

Key CRM Features

1. **Contact Management**: A CRM centralizes all contact information, making it easier to track interactions and communications with customers.

2. **Sales Automation**: Automates processes such as lead follow-up, opportunity management, and contract closure, improving the sales team's efficiency.

3. **Sales Pipeline**: Visualizes the lead's journey through the sales funnel, helping teams identify where leads are and what actions to take to advance them in the buying process.

4. **Reporting and Analytics**: Provides detailed reports on sales and marketing activities, allowing performance monitoring and identifying areas for improvement.

5. **Integration with Other Tools**: CRMs integrate with other marketing and sales platforms, such as email marketing, marketing automation, and social media management tools.

Main CRM Platforms

1. **Salesforce**: One of the most popular and comprehensive CRMs, Salesforce offers a wide range of features for contact management, sales automation, data analysis, and integration with other applications.

2. **HubSpot CRM**: Free and easy to use, HubSpot CRM provides tools for contact management, sales pipeline, marketing

automation, and integration with other HubSpot solutions.

3. **Zoho CRM**: Offers advanced features for contact management, sales pipeline, marketing automation, and data analysis, with a strong emphasis on customization and integration.

4. **Pipedrive**: With an intuitive and sales-focused interface, Pipedrive helps teams manage sales opportunities and maintain control over the entire sales process.

Marketing Automation Platforms

Definition and Importance

Marketing automation platforms allow repetitive marketing activities to be automated, improving campaign efficiency and personalizing communications with potential customers. These tools are essential for lead generation because they enable scaling marketing activities and maintaining constant engagement with the target audience.

Key Features of Marketing Automation Platforms

1. **Email Automation**: Allows the creation and sending of automatic email campaigns based on specific triggers, such as newsletter subscription or contact form completion.

2. **Lead Scoring**: Evaluates leads based on their behavior and interactions with the brand, helping identify the most promising leads and prioritize follow-up activities.

3. **Audience Segmentation**: Divides the audience into segments based on demographic data, behaviors, and interests, allowing for more targeted and relevant messages.

4. **Landing Pages and Forms**: Enables the creation of customized landing pages and contact forms to capture visitor information and convert them into leads.

5. **Analytics and Reporting**: Provides detailed data on marketing campaign performance, allowing key metrics to be monitored and marketing strategies optimized.

Main Marketing Automation Platforms

1. **HubSpot Marketing Hub**: Offers a complete suite of marketing automation tools, including email marketing, lead scoring, segmentation, landing page creation, and advanced analytics.

2. **Marketo**: A powerful and versatile marketing automation solution with advanced features for lead management, campaign automation, and data analysis.

3. **Pardot**: Part of the Salesforce suite, Pardot is designed for B2B marketing needs, with tools for email automation, lead scoring, segmentation, and campaign analysis.

4. **ActiveCampaign**: Combines marketing automation, CRM, and email marketing, offering an integrated solution for contact management, campaign automation, and data analysis.

Analytics and Reporting Tools

Definition and Importance

Analytics and reporting tools are essential for measuring the effectiveness of lead generation strategies, monitoring campaign performance, and making data-driven decisions. These tools allow detailed data on marketing and sales activities to be collected, analyzed, and visualized, helping identify improvement areas and optimize lead generation strategies.

Key Features of Analytics and Reporting Tools

1. **Conversion Tracking**: Monitors conversions generated by different marketing activities, helping understand which strategies are most effective in generating leads.

2. **Web Traffic Analysis**: Provides detailed data on website traffic, including the number of visitors, pages visited, time spent on the site, and traffic sources.

3. **Campaign Monitoring**: Tracks marketing campaign performance, allowing key metrics like email open rates, click-through rates, and conversion rates to be analyzed.

4. **Custom Dashboards**: Creates custom

dashboards that clearly and intuitively display the most important metrics, making it easier to understand data and share information with the team.

5. **Detailed Reports**: Generates detailed reports on marketing and sales activities, providing a complete view of performance and areas for improvement.

Main Analytics and Reporting Tools

1. **Google Analytics**: One of the most widely used web analytics tools, Google Analytics offers a wide range of features for web traffic tracking, conversion analysis, and detailed reporting.

2. **Tableau**: A business intelligence platform that allows complex data to be visualized and analyzed through interactive dashboards and custom reports.

3. **Mixpanel**: A product analytics tool that tracks and analyzes user interactions with digital products, providing detailed insights into user behavior.

4. **Kissmetrics**: Provides detailed customer behavior analytics, helping companies understand how users interact with the website and optimize marketing strategies.

5. **Hotjar**: A user behavior analytics tool offering features like heatmaps, session recordings, and surveys to gather feedback on websites.

Social Media Management

Definition and Importance

Social media management is crucial for lead generation because social platforms offer a direct channel to interact with the audience, build relationships, and promote content. Social media management tools help plan, publish, and monitor social activities, improving the effectiveness of social media marketing strategies.

Key Features of Social Media Management Tools

1. **Planning and Scheduling**: Allows posts to be planned and scheduled on social media in advance, ensuring a constant and consistent presence on all platforms.

2. **Performance Monitoring**: Tracks key performance metrics on social media, such as engagement, reach, clicks, and conversions, helping evaluate campaign effectiveness.

3. **Interaction Management**: Centralizes the management of interactions with followers, allowing efficient responses to comments, messages, and mentions.

4. **Competitor Analysis**: Provides insights into competitors' activities on social media, allowing winning strategies to be identified and own tactics adapted accordingly.

5. **Report Creation**: Generates detailed reports on social media activities and performance, making it easier to share information with the team and evaluate strategies.

Main Social Media Management Tools

1. **Hootsuite**: One of the most popular social media management platforms, Hootsuite offers planning, monitoring, analysis, and interaction management features on all major social platforms.

2. **Buffer**: Facilitates planning and scheduling social media posts, offering performance analysis and report creation features.

3. **Sprout Social**: A comprehensive social media management solution, Sprout Social offers advanced tools for planning, monitoring, analysis, and interaction management.

4. **SocialBee**: A tool that allows creating and scheduling content on social media, with features for managing content categories and performance monitoring.

5. **AgoraPulse**: Provides tools for social media planning, monitoring, and analysis, with additional features for managing contests and creating detailed reports.

Lead generation requires the integration and effective use of various tools and platforms that support every stage of the process, from contact management to campaign planning, performance analysis, and social media interaction management. By using CRM, marketing automation platforms, analytics and reporting tools, and social media management tools, companies can optimize their lead generation strategies, improve campaign efficiency, and increase conversion rates, ensuring sustainable and successful growth.

5.Analysis and Measurement of Results

Analyzing and measuring results are essential for evaluating the effectiveness of lead generation strategies and making data-driven decisions to improve future campaigns. This section will explore the Key Performance Indicators (KPIs) for lead generation, data analysis techniques, and campaign monitoring, providing a comprehensive overview of how companies can optimize their marketing and sales activities.

KPIs for Lead Generation

Definition of KPIs

KPIs, or Key Performance Indicators, are quantifiable metrics that help measure the success of an organization or specific activity. In the context of lead generation, KPIs are used to evaluate the effectiveness of marketing campaigns and sales strategies in generating new qualified contacts that can be converted into customers.

Main KPIs for Lead Generation

1. **Number of Leads Generated**: The total number of new leads acquired within a specific period. This KPI is a basic measure of the effectiveness of lead generation activities.

2. **Marketing Qualified Leads (MQL)**: Leads that have shown significant interest in the company's products or services and have been qualified by the marketing team as ready to be passed to the sales team.

3. **Sales Qualified Leads (SQL)**: Leads that have been further qualified by the sales team and are considered ready for a potential sales conversation.

4. **Lead Conversion Rate**: The percentage

of leads that convert into actual customers. This KPI measures the overall effectiveness of the sales funnel.

5. **Cost per Lead (CPL)**: The total cost of marketing and advertising activities divided by the number of leads generated. This KPI helps evaluate the efficiency of marketing expenditures.

6. **Average Conversion Time**: The average time between when a lead is generated and when it is converted into a customer. This KPI measures the speed of the sales funnel.

7. **Customer Lifetime Value (CLV)**: The estimated total profit a company can expect to obtain from a customer throughout the entire duration of the customer relationship. This KPI is essential for understanding the long-term value of generated leads.

8. **Return on Investment (ROI) of Lead Generation Campaigns**: The ratio of profit generated by lead generation campaigns to the cost of the campaigns. This KPI is crucial for assessing the economic effectiveness of marketing campaigns.

9. **Lead Engagement**: Metrics that measure the level of interaction of leads with the company's content, such as email open rates, click-through rates, time spent on the website, and social media interactions.

10. **Lead Churn Rate**: The percentage of leads that drop out of the sales funnel or become inactive. A high churn rate may indicate issues with lead quality or nurturing strategies.

Data Analysis Techniques

Importance of Data Analysis

Data analysis is crucial for understanding the performance of lead generation campaigns and making informed decisions to improve marketing and sales strategies. Through data analysis, companies can identify trends, discover optimization opportunities, and measure the impact of their activities.

Main Data Analysis Techniques

1. **Descriptive Analysis**: Provides an overview of historical data to understand what has happened. It uses techniques like data visualization, charts, and tables to present key information on the performance of lead generation campaigns.

2. **Diagnostic Analysis**: Explores data to determine why certain events occurred. It uses correlation and regression techniques to identify the causes of campaign successes or failures.

3. **Predictive Analysis**: Uses statistical models and machine learning algorithms to predict future trends and behaviors. This technique helps identify which leads are more likely to convert and which strategies might be more effective in the future.

4. **Prescriptive Analysis**: Provides specific recommendations on what actions to take to optimize performance. It uses advanced models and simulations to suggest the best marketing and sales strategies.

5. **Lead Segmentation**: Divides leads into homogeneous groups based on common characteristics such as demographics, behavior, preferences, and engagement levels. Segmentation helps customize nurturing strategies and improve conversion rates.

6. **Sales Funnel Analysis**: Examines the path of leads through the sales funnel to identify drop-off points and improvement opportunities. This technique helps optimize

the sales process and reduce average conversion time.

7. **Cohort Analysis**: Analyzes groups of leads that share similar characteristics or were generated in the same period. This technique helps understand lead behavior over time and assess the impact of marketing campaigns.

8. **Multichannel Campaign Analysis**: Evaluates the effectiveness of lead generation campaigns across different marketing channels, such as email, social media, SEO, SEM, and events. This technique helps determine which channels generate the most qualified leads and the best ROI.

Campaign Monitoring

Importance of Campaign Monitoring

Monitoring campaigns is essential for real-time evaluation of marketing activities and making quick, informed adjustments to strategies. Effective monitoring allows for timely identification of underperforming campaigns and optimization of those generating positive results.

Tools and Techniques for Campaign Monitoring

1. **Marketing Automation Platforms**: Tools like HubSpot, Marketo, and Pardot offer advanced functionalities for campaign monitoring, including real-time dashboards, performance analysis, and detailed reporting.

2. **Google Analytics**: Provides detailed data on the performance of digital marketing campaigns, including website traffic, user behavior, conversions, and key campaign metrics.

3. **Social Media Monitoring Tools**:

Platforms like Hootsuite, Buffer, and Sprout Social enable monitoring of social media campaign performance, including engagement, reach, clicks, and conversions.

4. **CRM Software**: Tools like Salesforce, Zoho CRM, and HubSpot CRM offer functionalities for tracking sales and marketing activities, including lead tracking, opportunity management, and sales team performance analysis.

5. **Email Marketing Platforms**: Tools like Mailchimp, Constant Contact, and ActiveCampaign allow monitoring of email campaign performance, including open rates, click-through rates, conversions, and overall engagement.

6. **A/B Testing**: A monitoring technique that involves creating two or more versions of a campaign to test which version yields the best results. A/B testing is useful for optimizing campaign elements such as

content, images, CTAs, and sending times.

7. **Heatmaps and User Behavior Analysis**: Tools like Hotjar and Crazy Egg provide detailed visualizations of user behavior on the website, including clicks, scrolling, and mouse movements. These insights help understand how leads interact with website content and identify areas for improvement.

8. **Tracking Pixels and UTM Codes**: Used to track the performance of advertising and digital marketing campaigns. Tracking pixels and UTM codes allow for monitoring lead behavior and properly attributing conversions to different marketing channels.

Analyzing and measuring results are critical components of lead generation. By utilizing KPIs, advanced data analysis techniques, and campaign monitoring tools, companies can evaluate the effectiveness of their marketing and sales strategies, identify optimization opportunities, and make informed decisions that enhance overall performance.

6.Analysis and Measurement of Results for Lead Generation Optimization

Analysis and measurement of results are fundamental for optimizing lead generation. These processes enable companies to evaluate the effectiveness of their marketing strategies, identify areas for improvement, and implement changes based on concrete data. To maximize the impact of lead generation campaigns, it is crucial not only to monitor performance but also to apply continuous optimization techniques such as A/B testing and continuous improvement practices. In this section, we will explore in detail how to analyze and measure results to optimize lead generation, with a particular focus on A/B testing and continuous improvement techniques.

Analysis and Measurement of Results

Importance of Analysis and Measurement

Analyzing and measuring results are essential for understanding the effectiveness of lead generation strategies and making data-driven adjustments. Without accurate evaluation, it is challenging to identify improvement areas and optimize campaigns. The key focus areas include:

1. **Campaign Performance Evaluation**: Measuring the effectiveness of campaigns in terms of lead generation and return on investment (ROI).

2. **Trend Identification**: Analyzing data to identify emerging trends and lead behaviors.

3. **Strategy Optimization**: Using data to make adjustments to marketing and sales strategies, continuously improving performance.

4. **Resource Allocation**: Determining which channels and tactics are most effective to allocate resources more efficiently.

Key KPIs for Lead Generation

To effectively evaluate lead generation campaigns, it is essential to monitor various Key Performance Indicators (KPIs). Some of the main KPIs include:

1. **Number of Leads Generated**: Indicates the total volume of leads acquired. It is a direct measure of the reach of marketing campaigns.

2. **Marketing Qualified Leads (MQL)**: Leads that have shown significant interest and are deemed ready for follow-up by the sales team.

3. **Sales Qualified Leads (SQL)**: Leads that have been further evaluated and considered ready for a sales proposal.

4. **Lead Conversion Rate**: The percentage of leads that become actual customers. This KPI measures the effectiveness of the sales funnel.

5. **Cost per Lead (CPL)**: The average cost to acquire a lead. It helps evaluate the efficiency of marketing expenditures.

6. **Average Conversion Time**: The

average time required to convert a lead into a customer. This KPI helps understand the speed of the sales process.

7. **Customer Lifetime Value (CLV)**: The estimated total value of a customer over the course of their relationship with the company. It allows assessing the profitability of leads.

8. **Lead Generation Campaign ROI**: The return on investment of marketing campaigns. It measures the overall profitability of lead generation activities.

9. **Lead Engagement**: Measures lead interaction with content and campaigns, including email open rates, clicks, and time spent on content.

10. **Lead Churn Rate**: The percentage of leads that drop out of the sales funnel or become inactive.

A/B Testing

What is A/B Testing?

A/B testing is an optimization technique that

involves creating two or more versions of an element (such as a landing page, email, or ad) to compare which version achieves better results. This method allows for data-driven decisions rather than relying on intuition or assumptions.

Steps of A/B Testing

1. **Defining Objectives**: Establish what you intend to improve with the test. For example, the goal might be to increase the conversion rate of a landing page.

2. **Creating Variants**: Develop two or more versions of the element to be tested, with targeted changes on specific aspects (such as design, text, or CTA).

3. **Segmenting the Audience**: Divide the audience into random groups and assign each group one of the variants. It is important that the groups are similar to obtain accurate results.

4. **Implementing the Test**: Launch the variants simultaneously and monitor the

performance of each version.

5. **Collecting Data**: Gather data on the performance of different variants in relation to the set objectives.

6. **Analyzing Results**: Compare the performance of the variants using key metrics, such as conversion rate, click-through rate (CTR), or average time spent.

7. **Implementing Changes**: Apply the changes based on the test results to optimize the tested element.

Examples of A/B Testing Applications

1. **Landing Pages**: Testing different versions of a landing page to determine which design or text generates the most conversions.

2. **Email Marketing**: Comparing different subject lines or email content to discover which versions have the highest open and click rates.

3. **Advertising Campaigns**: Testing various headlines, descriptions, or images in

ads to identify which elements attract the most attention and generate clicks.

4. **Call-to-Action (CTA)**: Testing different formulations and positions of CTAs to understand which version most effectively encourages users to complete a desired action.

Continuous Improvement Techniques

What is Continuous Improvement?

Continuous improvement is a systematic approach to continuously improving processes, products, and services. It is based on the idea that there are always opportunities to optimize performance and achieve better results. Continuous improvement techniques are essential for refining lead generation strategies and ensuring that campaigns are always cutting-edge and highly effective.

Continuous Improvement Techniques

1. **Feedback Analysis**: Collecting and

analyzing feedback from leads and customers to identify improvement areas. This can include surveys, reviews, and interviews.

2. **Process Review**: Examining and optimizing lead generation and sales processes to eliminate inefficiencies and improve effectiveness. This may involve simplifying workflows or introducing new technologies.

3. **Benchmarking**: Comparing the performance of your campaigns with those of competitors or industry best practices. Benchmarking helps identify improvement areas and set realistic goals.

4. **Advanced Technology Implementation**: Adopting new technologies and tools to enhance lead generation and marketing campaigns. This may include using artificial intelligence, machine learning, and predictive analytics.

5. **Team Training and Development**: Investing in the continuous training of the marketing and sales team to ensure they are up-to-date with the latest lead generation trends and techniques.

6. **Data-Driven Optimization**: Using data

collected from campaigns to make informed, results-based adjustments. This approach ensures decisions are supported by concrete evidence.

7. **Deming Cycle (PDCA)**: Applying the Plan-Do-Check-Act (PDCA) cycle to continuously improve processes. This approach involves planning changes, implementing them, monitoring results, and adjusting strategies.

8. **Iteration and Adaptation**: Adopting an iterative approach to improvement, making gradual changes, and monitoring results. This allows for quick adaptation of strategies based on market changes and lead responses.

9. **Root Cause Analysis**: Identifying the underlying causes of problems or inefficiencies using techniques like the Ishikawa diagram (fishbone diagram) or the 5 Whys method. This helps solve problems more effectively and prevent their recurrence.

10. **Customer Experience Improvement**: Optimizing the customer experience to increase satisfaction and loyalty. This can include personalizing communications,

improving customer service, and optimizing purchase pathways.

Analyzing and measuring results are crucial for optimizing lead generation. Monitoring KPIs, applying A/B testing, and implementing continuous improvement techniques enable companies to optimize their marketing campaigns and achieve better results. Using data-driven approaches, companies can identify improvement areas, adapt strategies, and ensure sustainable and successful growth. By integrating these practices into their marketing strategy, companies can gain a competitive advantage and maximize the value of lead generation.

7.Best Practices and Future Trends in Lead Generation

Lead generation is crucial for the success of any marketing and sales strategy. Adopting best practices and staying updated on emerging trends are essential to maximize the effectiveness of lead generation campaigns. This document explores best practices in market and lead generation, emerging innovations and technologies, and future predictions in lead generation.

Best Practices in Market and Lead Generation

1. **Understanding the Target Audience**

- **Creating Detailed Personas**: Define detailed profiles of ideal customers, known as personas. These personas should include demographic, behavioral, and psychographic information to create personalized content and messages.

- **Advanced Segmentation**: Segment the audience based on specific variables such as industry, role, interests, and behavior. This allows for more targeted and relevant campaigns.

2. **Offering Real Value**

- **Quality Content**: Create useful and informative content that addresses the audience's questions and problems. This can include blog articles, white papers, eBooks, infographics, and videos.

- **Lead Magnets**: Use lead magnets such as free guides, webinars, or free trials to incentivize users to provide their contact information.

3. **Optimizing Marketing Channels**

- **SEO and SEM**: Optimize content for search engines and invest in paid advertising to increase visibility and attract qualified leads.

- **Social Media Marketing**: Use social media to reach the target audience, promote content, and interact with potential leads. It is important to choose the right platforms based on the target audience.

- **Email Marketing**: Create personalized and segmented email marketing campaigns to nurture leads and guide them through the sales funnel.

4. **Implementing Advanced Technologies**

- **CRM and Marketing Automation**: Use

CRM and marketing automation tools to manage and nurture leads more efficiently. These tools help segment leads, automate follow-ups, and personalize communications.

- **Data Analysis**: Monitor and analyze data to evaluate campaign performance and optimize strategies based on results.

5. **Continuous Measurement and Optimization**

- **KPIs and Metrics**: Monitor KPIs to evaluate the effectiveness of lead generation campaigns. Examples of KPIs include the number of leads generated, cost per lead, and conversion rate.

- **A/B Testing**: Perform A/B tests to optimize campaign elements, such as landing pages, emails, and ads.

- **Feedback and Adaptation**: Collect feedback from leads and customers to identify areas for improvement and adapt strategies accordingly.

Innovations and Emerging Technologies

1. **Artificial Intelligence (AI) and Machine Learning**

- **Campaign Automation**: AI can automate the creation and management of marketing campaigns, improving efficiency and personalization.

- **Predictive Analytics**: Use machine learning algorithms to predict future lead behaviors and identify the most promising leads. This helps focus resources on leads with the highest conversion potential.

- **Chatbots and Virtual Assistants**: AI-powered chatbots can interact with website visitors, answer frequently asked questions, and qualify leads 24/7.

2. **Data-Driven Marketing**

- **Advanced Personalization**: Use lead data to create highly personalized marketing experiences. This can include product recommendations based on interests and past behavior.

- **Real-Time Analytics**: Implement real-time analytics tools to monitor and quickly respond to changes in campaign performance.

3. **Omnichannel Marketing**

- **Channel Integration**: Create a cohesive experience for leads across all marketing channels. This includes integration between email, social media, website, and paid advertising.

- **Tracking and Attribution**: Use advanced technologies to track the lead journey across different channels and accurately attribute conversions.

4. **Augmented Reality (AR) and Virtual Reality (VR)**

- **Immersive Experiences**: Use AR and VR to create immersive marketing experiences that engage leads and improve understanding of products or services.

- **Virtual Demonstrations**: Offer virtual product demonstrations to allow leads to explore and interact with products in a more engaging way.

5. **Blockchain for Data Security**

- **Data Protection**: Use blockchain technology to ensure the security and transparency of lead data management, improving customer trust.

- **Authenticity Verification**: Implement blockchain solutions to verify the authenticity of leads and prevent fraud.

The Future of Lead Generation

1. **Advanced Automation and Personalization**

- **Real-Time Personalized Marketing**: The use of AI and machine learning will enable increasingly precise and real-time personalization of marketing communications, improving the relevance and effectiveness of campaigns.

- **Workflow Automation**: Automation technologies will continue to evolve, allowing for more sophisticated lead management and highly personalized automated communication.

2. **Integration of Emerging Technologies**

- **AI and Big Data**: The integration of AI with big data will provide deeper insights into lead behaviors and optimize marketing strategies more effectively.

- **IoT (Internet of Things)**: IoT will significantly impact lead generation, with the ability to collect valuable data from connected devices and use it to create more targeted offers.

3. **Immersive Marketing Experiences**

- **AR and VR**: The growing adoption of AR and VR will offer innovative opportunities to engage leads and provide more engaging and memorable marketing experiences.

- **Personalized Experiences**: Personalized experiences, thanks to the use of advanced technologies, will become the norm, with marketing campaigns responding in real-time to lead preferences and actions.

4. **Evolution of Privacy Regulations**

- **Compliance and Transparency**: With increasing privacy regulations, such as GDPR and CCPA, companies will need to adopt more transparent and compliant data collection and management practices.

- **Consent and Control**: Leads will have greater control over their data and its usage, and companies will need to adapt their marketing strategies to respect these regulations.

5. **Focus on Customer Experience**

- **Customer Experience (CX)**: The future of lead generation will increasingly focus on providing an exceptional customer experience. Companies will need to focus on customer satisfaction and retention, not just on generating new leads.

- **Personalized Service**: Personalized interactions and proactive customer service will become key elements in attracting and retaining leads.

Adopting best practices in lead generation and staying updated on innovations and emerging trends are essential to achieving optimal results in marketing campaigns. Best practices, such as a deep understanding of the target audience and the implementation of advanced technologies, help improve the effectiveness of lead generation strategies. Additionally, the adoption of emerging technologies such as AI, machine learning, and immersive experiences will shape the future of lead generation, offering innovative opportunities to engage and convert leads into loyal customers. Preparing for these evolutions and adopting a data-driven and customer-oriented approach will be crucial for long-term success in lead generation.

8.Lead Generation Tips

Lead generation is a fundamental process for driving sales and ensuring the growth of any business. Here are some detailed and practical tips to improve your lead generation strategy, categorized for easier implementation.

---

1. **Content Strategies**

1.1. **Creating Quality Content**

- **Informative Blogs**: Write blog articles that answer common questions and solve typical problems for your target audience. Providing value through detailed and well-researched content attracts attention and builds trust.

- **Ebooks and White Papers**: Create in-depth content like ebooks or white papers that require an action, such as email registration, for download. These documents can address complex topics and offer concrete solutions.

- **Infographics**: Design infographics that synthesize data and information in a visually appealing way. Infographics are shareable and can increase your brand's visibility.

1.2. **Multimedia Content**

- **Videos**: Produce informative videos, tutorials, or customer testimonials. Videos are highly engaging and can be used across various platforms, including social media and YouTube.

- **Webinars**: Host webinars on topics of interest to your audience. Webinars provide opportunities for real-time interactions and to gather participant information.

- **Podcasts**: Start a podcast on relevant topics in your industry. Podcasts can help you reach a wider audience and establish your brand's authority.

1.3. **Lead Magnets**

- **Checklists and Guides**: Offer practical checklists or guides as lead magnets to attract qualified leads. These tools can help users achieve specific goals or solve particular problems.

- **Online Tools and Calculators**: Provide tools or calculators that help users obtain personalized information or solve problems. For example, an ROI calculator can attract leads interested in a specific solution.

- **Templates and Templates**: Create useful templates or templates for your target audience. These can be documents, spreadsheets, or presentations that simplify a complex process.

---

2. **Website Optimization**

2.1. **Landing Page Design**

- **Clear Call-to-Action (CTA)**: Use visible and persuasive CTAs on your landing pages. CTAs should clearly indicate what is obtained in exchange for contact information.

- **Simple Registration Forms**: Keep registration forms short and simple. Requesting only essential information increases the chances of conversion.

- **Social Proof**: Add testimonials, reviews, or case studies to your landing pages to build trust and demonstrate the value of your product or service.

2.2. **SEO (Search Engine Optimization)**

- **Keyword Research**: Conduct in-depth keyword research to optimize your content and web pages for relevant search queries.

- **On-Page Optimization**: Ensure every page of your website is optimized with meta tags, descriptions, and high-quality content to improve search engine rankings.

- **Backlink Creation**: Acquire backlinks from authoritative sites to enhance your site's authority and increase visibility in search results.

2.3. **Speed and User Experience (UX)**

- **Speed Optimization**: Improve your website's loading speed to reduce bounce rates and enhance user experience.

- **Responsive Design**: Ensure your website is optimized for mobile devices. A responsive design improves accessibility and usability across all platforms.

- **Intuitive Navigation**: Implement clear and intuitive navigation to make it easy for users to find information and reduce the time needed to complete desired actions.

---

3. **Social Media and Digital Marketing**

3.1. **Social Media Marketing**

- **Targeted Advertising Campaigns**: Use advanced targeting options on social media platforms to reach your ideal audience with sponsored ads.

- **Shareable Content**: Create content that encourages sharing on social media. High-quality, emotional, or provocative content tends to generate more engagement.

- **Engagement and Community Building**: Interact with your audience on social media by responding to comments and messages. Building an active community can lead to greater trust and more effective lead generation.

3.2. **Paid Advertising**

- **PPC (Pay-Per-Click) Campaigns**: Implement PPC campaigns on Google Ads and other platforms to attract qualified leads. Use keyword-based targeting and campaign optimization for the best results.

- **Remarketing**: Use remarketing strategies to reach users who visited your website but did not complete an action. Remarketing keeps your brand in front of potential leads and encourages their return.

- **LinkedIn Ads**: Utilize LinkedIn's advertising options to reach professionals and businesses, particularly useful for B2B.

3.3. **Email Marketing**

- **List Segmentation**: Segment your email list to send personalized and relevant content to different groups of leads.

- **Lead Nurturing Campaigns**: Create automated email sequences to nurture leads through the sales funnel, providing useful content and targeted promotions.

- **A/B Testing for Emails**: Conduct A/B tests on email subject lines, content, and CTAs to optimize your email campaign performance.

---

4. **Events and Networking**

4.1. **Trade Shows and Conferences**

- **Trade Show Participation**: Attend industry trade shows to meet potential leads and gather contacts. Prepare attractive marketing materials and offer live demonstrations.

- **Event Organization**: Organize your own events, such as workshops or seminars, to attract leads interested in your industry and services.

- **Active Networking**: Attend networking events and connect with other industry professionals to expand your contact network and generate new lead opportunities.

4.2. **Webinars and Live Streaming**

- **Webinar Organization**: Plan and

promote webinars on relevant topics for your audience. Use webinars as a tool to educate and qualify leads.

- **Live Q&A Sessions**: Offer live Q&A sessions to engage the audience and answer specific questions. This can help build trust and interest in your products or services.

- **Event Streaming**: Stream live events on social media or your website to reach a wider audience and gather interested contacts.

---

5. **Collaborations and Partnerships**

5.1. **Collaborations with Influencers**

- **Influencer Marketing**: Collaborate with industry influencers to promote your brand and reach new audience segments. Influencers can amplify your message and attract qualified leads.

- **Co-Creation of Content**: Work with influencers to create joint content, such as articles, videos, or social media posts, to leverage their audience and generate leads.

5.2. **Strategic Partnerships**

- **Collaborations with Complementary Companies**: Partner with companies offering complementary products or services to generate joint leads through cross-promotions or shared events.

- **Guest Blogging and Co-Branding**: Write articles for third-party blogs or participate in co-branding initiatives to increase your visibility and attract new leads.

- **Affiliate Programs**: Implement an affiliate program to incentivize external partners to promote your products or services and generate leads in exchange for commissions.

---

6. **Sales Funnel Optimization**

6.1. **Lead Scoring**

- **Lead Scoring Implementation**: Use lead scoring to evaluate and rank leads based on their quality and likelihood to convert. This helps focus resources on the most promising leads.

- **Personalization of Offers**: Tailor offers and communications based on lead scores to increase the chances of conversion.

6.2. **Customer Relationship Management (CRM)**

- **Lead Management with CRM**: Use a CRM to manage and track leads through the sales funnel. CRM helps keep track of interactions and optimize follow-up strategies.

- **Sales Process Automation**: Implement automation in CRM to streamline follow-up activities and improve efficiency in lead management.

6.3. **Analysis and Optimization**

- **Monitoring Conversion Metrics**: Analyze conversion metrics to evaluate the effectiveness of your lead generation strategies and make improvements.

- **Customer Feedback**: Collect feedback from customers and leads to identify areas for improvement and optimize acquisition and conversion strategies.

---

7. **Experimentation and Innovation**

7.1. **A/B Testing**

- **Testing Site Elements**: Perform A/B tests on website elements, such as headlines,

CTAs, and landing page layouts, to determine which variants generate more leads.

- **Testing Offers and Promotions**: Test different offers and promotions to identify which are most effective in converting leads into customers.

7.2. **Content Innovation**

- **Using Augmented Reality (AR)**: Implement AR to create engaging and interactive experiences that capture leads' attention and offer added value.

- **Implementing Artificial Intelligence (AI)**: Use AI to personalize communications and improve the effectiveness of marketing campaigns through predictive analysis and advanced segmentation.

---

8. **Retargeting Strategies**

8.1. **Web Retargeting**

- **Retargeting Campaigns**: Implement retargeting campaigns to reach website visitors who did not complete an action. Use targeted ads to bring them back to the site and encourage conversion.

- **Visitor Segmentation**: Segment website visitors based on their behavior and actions to create more personalized retargeting campaigns.

8.2. **Social Media Retargeting**

- **Retargeting Ads on Social Media**: Use social media retargeting options to reach users who interacted with your content or visited your profile.

- **Creating Suitable Content**: Develop specific content for social media retargeting campaigns to attract attention and encourage action.

---

9. **Data Management and Analysis**

9.1. **Monitoring KPIs**

- **Defining KPIs**: Establish and monitor relevant KPIs (Key Performance Indicators), such as cost per lead, conversion rate, and customer value, to assess the effectiveness of your lead generation strategies.

- **Analyzing Results**: Use analytics tools to examine data and identify areas for improvement in lead generation.

9.2. **Using Analytics Tools**

- **Google Analytics**: Implement Google Analytics to monitor

website traffic and analyze visitor behavior to

optimize lead generation campaigns.

- **Heatmap and Behavior Analysis**: Use heatmap tools to visualize user behavior on the website and identify areas of interest and potential improvement.

Implementing an effective lead generation strategy requires a multifaceted approach that combines high-quality content, website optimization, social media use, and technological innovations. The tips provided above offer a wide range of techniques and strategies that can be tailored to the specific needs of your company and industry. Constantly monitoring results, testing new ideas, and optimizing your campaigns based on data will allow you to continually improve your lead generation and achieve your marketing and sales goals.

Index

8.Lead Generation Tips pg.96